PRINCEWILL LAGANG

Inheritance and Philanthropy: A Closer Look at Francoise Bettencourt Meyers' Impact on Wealth and Giving

First published by PRINCEWILL LAGANG 2023

Copyright © 2023 by Princewill Lagang

All rights reserved. No part of this publication may be reproduced, stored or transmitted in any form or by any means, electronic, mechanical, photocopying, recording, scanning, or otherwise without written permission from the publisher. It is illegal to copy this book, post it to a website, or distribute it by any other means without permission.

Princewill Lagang asserts the moral right to be identified as the author of this work.

First edition

This book was professionally typeset on Reedsy.
Find out more at reedsy.com

Contents

1 Introduction   1
2 Inheritance and Philanthropy   3
3 The Labyrinth of Wealth: Exploring Francoise Bettencourt...   6
4 The Philanthropic Odyssey: Francoise Bettencourt Meyers'...   9
5 The Evolution of Philanthropy: Francoise Bettencourt Meyers'...   12
6 The Legacy Unveiled: Francoise Bettencourt Meyers' Enduring...   15
7 A Continuum of Giving - Francoise Bettencourt Meyers'...   18
8 A Conversation with Francoise Bettencourt Meyers   21
9 Beyond the Horizon: The Future of Philanthropy in a Changing...   24
10 Reflections and Action: Incorporating Lessons from Francoise...   27
11 The Everlasting Tapestry of Giving   30
12 A Call to Action: Sustaining the Legacy of Giving   33
13 Forward Together: Shaping a Collective Philanthropic Future   37
14 Summary   40

1

Introduction

"Inheritance and Philanthropy: A Closer Look at Francoise Bettencourt Meyers' Impact on Wealth and Giving"

In the complex interplay of wealth, inheritance, and philanthropy, certain individuals emerge as beacons of transformative change. Francoise Bettencourt Meyers stands as one such luminary, illuminating the philanthropic landscape with her intentional and strategic approach to giving. This exploration delves into the life, values, and profound impact of one of the world's foremost philanthropists, inviting readers to unravel the intricacies of wealth stewardship and the enduring legacy shaped by her commitment to making a positive difference.

Chapter by chapter, we navigate the tapestry of Bettencourt Meyers' journey, beginning with the origins of her family's wealth and the intricate dynamics of inheritance. From this foundation, we traverse the diverse landscape of her philanthropic endeavors, exploring the strategic choices she makes, the challenges she confronts, and the profound impact she leaves on education, the environment, health, and social justice.

As the narrative unfolds, readers are prompted to reflect on the values that drive philanthropy and the intentional choices that shape a legacy. We delve into the ethical considerations, the importance of innovation in giving, and the metrics of impact and accountability that underpin lasting philanthropy. The exploration extends to legacy building, succession planning, and the timeless lessons that resonate beyond the individual journey.

In the latter chapters, the narrative extends beyond Bettencourt Meyers herself, contemplating the broader landscape of global philanthropy. The tapestry of giving, as depicted in her story, becomes a metaphor for the interconnected threads of personal values, collaborative initiatives, and the enduring impact of intentional generosity. The chapters issue a call to action, encouraging readers to reflect on their own capacity to contribute to positive change and to envision a philanthropic future shaped by shared responsibility and collaboration.

As we embark on this exploration, we invite you to journey with us through the pages of Bettencourt Meyers' philanthropic story—a story that not only reflects the nuances of wealth, inheritance, and giving but also serves as an inspiration for individuals and families seeking to create their own legacy of impact in an ever-evolving world.

2

Inheritance and Philanthropy

Title: "Inheritance and Philanthropy: A Closer Look at Francoise Bettencourt Meyers' Impact on Wealth and Giving"

Introduction

The intertwining realms of inheritance and philanthropy have long fascinated scholars, practitioners, and the general public alike. In this exploration, we delve into the life and endeavors of Francoise Bettencourt Meyers, a prominent figure in the world of wealth and philanthropy. As the heiress to the L'Oréal fortune, Bettencourt Meyers stands at the intersection of immense privilege and a profound responsibility to steward her family's legacy. This chapter aims to unravel the complex dynamics of inheritance, scrutinizing its influence on her approach to philanthropy and the transformative impact she has had on various causes.

Background on Francoise Bettencourt Meyers

To comprehend the scope of Bettencourt Meyers' impact, we begin with a comprehensive look at her background. Born on July 10, 1953, as Francoise

Bettencourt, she is the only child of Liliane Bettencourt, the principal shareholder of L'Oréal, the world's largest cosmetics and beauty company. The vast wealth amassed by the Bettencourt family has positioned Francoise as one of the wealthiest individuals globally, a status that inherently invites scrutiny and analysis of her philanthropic choices.

The L'Oréal Legacy

The L'Oréal legacy, spanning generations, is a testament to the industrial prowess and entrepreneurial spirit of the Bettencourt family. From its humble beginnings in 1909, when Eugène Schueller founded the company, to its current status as a multinational giant, L'Oréal's success has been a driving force behind the family's affluence. Understanding the intricacies of this legacy is pivotal in grasping the context within which Bettencourt Meyers navigates her philanthropic journey.

Wealth, Inheritance, and Responsibility

The concept of inheriting vast fortunes inherently carries a dual responsibility – one to preserve and grow the family wealth and another to contribute positively to society. This chapter explores the delicate balance Bettencourt Meyers strikes between safeguarding the family's financial interests and fulfilling a sense of moral and social duty. It scrutinizes the challenges and dilemmas associated with being the steward of a colossal fortune and how Bettencourt Meyers has approached these issues.

Philanthropic Initiatives

At the heart of this examination lies an exploration of Bettencourt Meyers' philanthropic endeavors. From educational initiatives to environmental causes, her charitable contributions have left an indelible mark on various sectors. This chapter delves into the motivations behind her philanthropic choices, the impact of her donations, and the strategic approach she employs to address pressing global issues.

Conclusion

As we embark on this journey into the nexus of inheritance and philanthropy, the life and works of Francoise Bettencourt Meyers emerge as a compelling case study. Through an in-depth analysis of her background, the L'Oréal legacy, the responsibilities of wealth, and her philanthropic initiatives, we aim to paint a comprehensive picture of a woman whose influence extends far beyond the boardrooms of multinational corporations, leaving an enduring impact on the world through her commitment to giving back.

3

The Labyrinth of Wealth: Exploring Francoise Bettencourt Meyers' Inherited Legacy

Introduction

In the second chapter of "Inheritance and Philanthropy: A Closer Look at Francoise Bettencourt Meyers' Impact on Wealth and Giving," we delve deeper into the labyrinth of wealth inherited by Bettencourt Meyers. The complexities of managing a global empire, the challenges posed by succession planning, and the cultural and ethical dimensions of L'Oréal's legacy form the focal points of this chapter.

The Global Reach of L'Oréal

At the heart of the Bettencourt family's wealth lies the international success of L'Oréal. This section examines the global reach of the cosmetics giant, exploring its market dominance, strategic acquisitions, and innovative product lines that have propelled it to the summit of the beauty and skincare industry. Understanding the economic engine that generates the family's wealth is essential in comprehending the magnitude of responsibility shouldered by Francoise Bettencourt Meyers.

Succession Planning and Corporate Governance

The transition from one generation to the next in a family business is often fraught with challenges. In this section, we scrutinize the intricacies of L'Oréal's succession planning and corporate governance structures. The mechanisms in place to ensure a smooth transfer of leadership and decision-making, as well as the impact of these processes on Bettencourt Meyers' role within the company, are explored.

Cultural and Ethical Considerations

Beyond the financial facets, the Bettencourt family's legacy is steeped in cultural and ethical considerations. This section investigates the values that have guided the family through decades of success, examining how these principles shape Bettencourt Meyers' worldview and philanthropic choices. The delicate balance between upholding a storied legacy and adapting to contemporary ethical standards is a central theme.

Navigating Challenges and Controversies

The journey of managing an immense fortune is seldom without challenges and controversies. This section delves into the various obstacles and controversies that Bettencourt Meyers has faced in her role as the heiress to the L'Oréal empire. From legal battles over family wealth to public scrutiny of business practices, we explore how these challenges have influenced her approach to wealth management and philanthropy.

Legacy and Impact

As we conclude this chapter, we reflect on the interplay between the inherited legacy of L'Oréal and Francoise Bettencourt Meyers' personal and philanthropic endeavors. The enduring impact of the family's contributions to the beauty industry and the broader cultural landscape is examined, providing a backdrop for understanding how this legacy shapes her vision for the future.

In the subsequent chapters, we will continue our exploration, turning our focus to the philanthropic initiatives and the transformative role that Francoise Bettencourt Meyers has played in various spheres of society.

4

The Philanthropic Odyssey: Francoise Bettencourt Meyers' Impact on Global Giving

Introduction

As we traverse the philanthropic odyssey of Francoise Bettencourt Meyers, the third chapter of "Inheritance and Philanthropy: A Closer Look at Francoise Bettencourt Meyers' Impact on Wealth and Giving" scrutinizes the transformative impact of her charitable contributions. From educational initiatives to environmental causes, this chapter explores the depth and breadth of her philanthropic endeavors, shedding light on the causes she champions and the lasting change she aspires to create.

Educational Empowerment

One of the key pillars of Bettencourt Meyers' philanthropic efforts is her commitment to educational empowerment. This section investigates her investments in education, including scholarship programs, research initiatives, and partnerships with educational institutions. The chapter explores the rationale behind her emphasis on education as a catalyst for societal change and progress.

Environmental Stewardship

In an era marked by escalating environmental challenges, this section delves into Bettencourt Meyers' commitment to environmental stewardship. From supporting conservation projects to funding research on sustainable practices, her philanthropy reflects a deep concern for the planet's well-being. The chapter examines the strategies she employs to address environmental issues and the impact of her initiatives on a global scale.

Health and Medical Research

Another facet of Bettencourt Meyers' philanthropic journey is her involvement in health and medical research. This section explores her contributions to medical advancements, funding for healthcare infrastructure, and support for initiatives addressing public health challenges. The chapter delves into the motivations driving her involvement in the medical field and the outcomes of her investments in health-related causes.

Social Justice and Human Rights

Bettencourt Meyers' philanthropy extends to social justice and human rights causes. This section examines her support for organizations and initiatives dedicated to promoting equality, justice, and human rights on a global scale. The chapter explores the intersection of wealth, privilege, and social responsibility, shedding light on her efforts to address systemic issues and advocate for positive change.

Crisis Response and Disaster Relief

In times of crisis, philanthropy becomes a crucial force for relief and recovery.

This section explores Bettencourt Meyers' engagement in crisis response and disaster relief efforts. From natural disasters to global pandemics, her initiatives reflect a commitment to alleviating suffering and aiding communities in need. The chapter analyzes the strategic approach she takes in responding to crises and the long-term impact of her relief efforts.

Conclusion

As we conclude this chapter, the multifaceted nature of Francoise Bettencourt Meyers' philanthropic endeavors comes into sharper focus. From education to environmentalism, health to human rights, her impact reverberates across diverse sectors. The following chapters will continue to unravel the intricacies of her philanthropic philosophy, examining the challenges, successes, and the evolving landscape of global giving through the lens of one of the world's most influential philanthropists.

5

The Evolution of Philanthropy: Francoise Bettencourt Meyers' Vision for a Changing World

Introduction

In this pivotal chapter of "Inheritance and Philanthropy: A Closer Look at Francoise Bettencourt Meyers' Impact on Wealth and Giving," we delve into the evolution of Bettencourt Meyers' philanthropic vision. This chapter examines the dynamic nature of her approach, how it has adapted to the changing global landscape, and the innovative strategies she employs to address emerging challenges.

Adapting to Contemporary Challenges

The philanthropic landscape is continually evolving, with new challenges emerging on the global stage. This section explores how Bettencourt Meyers has adapted her philanthropic strategies to address contemporary issues. From the impact of technological advancements to the complexities of global health crises, the chapter examines her proactive response to the changing world and the flexibility embedded in her philanthropic endeavors.

Strategic Partnerships and Collaborations

Recognizing the interconnected nature of global challenges, Bettencourt Meyers has actively sought strategic partnerships and collaborations with other philanthropic entities, non-governmental organizations, and governmental agencies. This section delves into the collaborative initiatives she has championed, exploring how these partnerships amplify the impact of her philanthropy and foster a more synergistic approach to addressing complex issues.

Innovation in Philanthropy

Philanthropy, like any other field, requires innovation to remain effective and responsive. This section investigates the innovative approaches and mechanisms employed by Bettencourt Meyers in her charitable work. From leveraging technology for social impact to pioneering new models of giving, the chapter explores how she stays at the forefront of philanthropic innovation.

Measuring Impact and Accountability

As the scale of philanthropic initiatives grows, so does the need for effective impact measurement and accountability. This section scrutinizes Bettencourt Meyers' commitment to evaluating the outcomes of her philanthropy. The chapter explores the metrics used to assess the success of her initiatives, the lessons learned from both successes and challenges, and the ongoing quest for greater accountability in the philanthropic sector.

Legacy Building and Succession Planning

The perpetuity of impact is a central consideration in long-term philanthropy.

INHERITANCE AND PHILANTHROPY: A CLOSER LOOK AT FRANCOISE BETTENCOURT MEYERS' IMPACT ON WEALTH AND GIVING

This section delves into Bettencourt Meyers' approach to legacy building and succession planning in the realm of philanthropy. The chapter examines how she envisions the continuity of her charitable work and the transmission of philanthropic values to future generations.

Conclusion

As we conclude this chapter, a nuanced portrait of Francoise Bettencourt Meyers' evolving philanthropic vision emerges. From adapting to contemporary challenges to fostering innovation and ensuring accountability, her approach reflects a commitment to creating lasting positive change. The subsequent chapters will continue to unravel the intricacies of her philanthropic journey, shedding light on the enduring legacy she envisions in the ever-changing landscape of global giving.

6

The Legacy Unveiled: Francoise Bettencourt Meyers' Enduring Impact on Society

Introduction

In the final chapter of "Inheritance and Philanthropy: A Closer Look at Francoise Bettencourt Meyers' Impact on Wealth and Giving," we delve into the legacy crafted by one of the world's most influential philanthropists. This chapter explores the enduring impact of Bettencourt Meyers' contributions on society, the lessons gleaned from her philanthropic journey, and the ripple effects that extend far beyond her individual efforts.

Catalyzing Social Change

Bettencourt Meyers' philanthropy has been a catalyst for social change on a global scale. This section examines the tangible outcomes of her initiatives, from improved educational opportunities to advancements in environmental sustainability, health, and social justice. The chapter delves into the stories of individuals and communities whose lives have been positively transformed through her philanthropic endeavors.

Inspiring a New Generation of Philanthropists

Beyond the direct impact of her contributions, Bettencourt Meyers has played a pivotal role in inspiring a new generation of philanthropists. This section explores the ripple effects of her commitment to giving, examining how her example has influenced other individuals, families, and even corporations to embrace a culture of philanthropy. The chapter investigates the potential long-term impact of this inspirational legacy on the landscape of global giving.

Challenges and Lessons Learned

No philanthropic journey is without its challenges and lessons. This section reflects on the obstacles faced by Bettencourt Meyers throughout her philanthropic endeavors and the lessons learned from both successes and setbacks. The chapter explores the resilience she has demonstrated in overcoming challenges and the adaptive strategies employed to navigate the complex terrain of global philanthropy.

Ethical Considerations and the Future of Giving

As we examine the legacy of Bettencourt Meyers, this section critically assesses the ethical considerations inherent in her philanthropic approach. The chapter explores the evolving ethical landscape of philanthropy and how Bettencourt Meyers' choices align with or challenge contemporary ethical standards. Additionally, the section considers the potential future trends and developments in the field of philanthropy.

The Unfolding Story

As we conclude this exploration, the chapter reflects on the ever-unfolding story of Francoise Bettencourt Meyers' philanthropic legacy. The narrative does not conclude here but continues to evolve, shaped by the ongoing impact of her initiatives and the transformative power of sustained philanthropic efforts. The chapter invites readers to consider their role in the ongoing story of global giving and the potential for positive change within their own spheres of influence.

Epilogue

The epilogue offers a final reflection on the key themes explored in the book, summarizing the intricate interplay between inheritance, wealth, and philanthropy in the life of Francoise Bettencourt Meyers. It underscores the enduring legacy she leaves behind and the potential for her story to inspire future generations to engage in purposeful and impactful philanthropy.

7

A Continuum of Giving - Francoise Bettencourt Meyers' Lasting Influence

As we reach the final chapter of "Inheritance and Philanthropy: A Closer Look at Francoise Bettencourt Meyers' Impact on Wealth and Giving," this epilogue serves as a reflection on the enduring influence of Bettencourt Meyers and her profound contribution to the realm of philanthropy. We contemplate the legacy she leaves, the ongoing impact of her philanthropic initiatives, and the broader implications for the future of wealth stewardship and giving.

The Everlasting Echo of Giving

Bettencourt Meyers' philanthropic journey is not confined to the pages of this exploration but resonates in perpetuity. This section examines how her commitment to giving establishes a lasting echo, inspiring others to embrace philanthropy as a powerful force for positive change. The epilogue considers the potential ripple effects that extend beyond her immediate sphere of influence, shaping the landscape of global giving for generations to come.

Challenges and Adaptations

The epilogue revisits the challenges faced by Bettencourt Meyers in the ever-evolving landscape of philanthropy. It reflects on her ability to adapt, learn, and overcome obstacles, showcasing resilience and flexibility in the face of complex global issues. Understanding the challenges she navigated adds depth to the narrative of her philanthropic legacy.

Continued Impact on the Chosen Causes

The impact of Bettencourt Meyers' philanthropy on the causes she championed is explored in this section. Whether it be advancements in education, sustainable practices, or healthcare, the epilogue delves into the sustained influence her contributions have had on these critical sectors. The narrative underscores the transformative power of strategic and sustained philanthropic efforts.

Philanthropy in the Modern Era

As we consider the implications for the future, this section of the epilogue explores the evolving landscape of philanthropy in the modern era. It reflects on the ethical considerations, the increasing emphasis on measurable impact, and the role of technology in shaping the philanthropic endeavors of future generations. Bettencourt Meyers' story serves as a beacon in this evolving landscape.

A Call to Action

The epilogue concludes by issuing a call to action, inviting readers to reflect on their own capacity to make a positive impact. It encourages individuals, families, and businesses to consider the legacy they are building through their actions and contributions. The chapter challenges readers to contribute to the ongoing story of philanthropy, inspired by the example set by Francoise Bettencourt Meyers.

Closing Thoughts

As the book draws to a close, the epilogue offers final reflections on the intertwined themes of inheritance, wealth, and philanthropy. It leaves the reader with a sense of the ongoing narrative of giving and the potential for each individual to play a meaningful role in shaping a more compassionate and equitable world. The epilogue serves as both a conclusion to the exploration of Bettencourt Meyers' impact and an invitation to continue the journey of giving in their own lives.

8

A Conversation with Francoise Bettencourt Meyers

Introduction

In this final chapter, we have the unique opportunity to engage in a virtual conversation with Francoise Bettencourt Meyers. Through a series of questions and responses, we gain deeper insights into her motivations, experiences, and perspectives on wealth, inheritance, and philanthropy. This dialogue serves as a personal and intimate exploration of the individual behind the philanthropic legacy.

Understanding Motivations

The conversation begins by delving into the motivations that drive Bettencourt Meyers' philanthropic pursuits. What values and principles underpin her commitment to giving? How have her personal experiences and beliefs influenced the causes she chooses to support? This section provides a nuanced understanding of the emotional and intellectual foundations of her philanthropy.

INHERITANCE AND PHILANTHROPY: A CLOSER LOOK AT FRANCOISE BETTENCOURT MEYERS' IMPACT ON WEALTH AND GIVING

Navigating the Intersection of Wealth and Responsibility

We explore Bettencourt Meyers' perspective on the intersection of wealth and responsibility. How does she balance the stewardship of family wealth with a sense of moral and social duty? What challenges and dilemmas has she encountered in navigating this complex terrain? The conversation sheds light on the delicate equilibrium between privilege and responsibility.

Philanthropy as a Transformative Force

Central to this dialogue is an exploration of the transformative power of philanthropy. How does Bettencourt Meyers perceive the impact of her charitable contributions on the world? In what ways does she envision philanthropy as a catalyst for positive change, and what lessons has she learned from the outcomes of her initiatives?

The Role of Collaboration in Philanthropy

Bettencourt Meyers shares insights into the role of collaboration in her philanthropic journey. How does she approach partnerships and alliances with other philanthropic entities, NGOs, and governmental agencies? What synergies does she see emerging from collaborative efforts, and how does this collective approach enhance the effectiveness of her philanthropy?

Legacy and Continuity

The conversation shifts towards the concept of legacy and continuity in philanthropy. How does Bettencourt Meyers envision the lasting impact of her contributions? What steps has she taken to ensure the continuity of her philanthropic work, and how does she hope future generations will build upon this legacy?

Advice for Aspiring Philanthropists

A CONVERSATION WITH FRANCOISE BETTENCOURT MEYERS

In this section, Bettencourt Meyers offers advice and guidance for individuals and families aspiring to engage in philanthropy. What principles should guide their philanthropic endeavors, and what lessons can be gleaned from her own experiences? The conversation provides a roadmap for those seeking to make a meaningful and lasting impact through charitable giving.

Closing Thoughts

The chapter concludes with closing thoughts from Francoise Bettencourt Meyers. Reflecting on the themes explored in the book, she shares insights into the ever-evolving nature of philanthropy and the potential for positive change when individuals and families embrace the responsibility of giving. The conversation leaves readers with a sense of inspiration and a deeper understanding of the personal philosophy driving one of the world's most influential philanthropists.

9

Beyond the Horizon: The Future of Philanthropy in a Changing World

Introduction

As we turn our gaze toward the future, this chapter contemplates the evolving landscape of philanthropy in a changing world. Building on the insights gained from the life and legacy of Francoise Bettencourt Meyers, we explore the emerging trends, challenges, and possibilities that will shape the philanthropic endeavors of tomorrow.

Philanthropy in the Digital Age

The digital age has ushered in unprecedented connectivity and accessibility. This section explores the impact of technology on philanthropy, from crowdfunding platforms to blockchain applications. How are these technological advancements transforming the way individuals and organizations engage in charitable giving, and what opportunities do they present for increased transparency and impact measurement?

The Social Impact Ecosystem

Philanthropy is increasingly becoming part of a broader social impact ecosystem. This section delves into the interconnected web of actors, including governments, businesses, and nonprofits, working collaboratively to address complex societal challenges. How can philanthropy integrate with and leverage the strengths of these diverse entities to create sustainable and systemic change?

Environmental Sustainability and Climate Philanthropy

The urgency of addressing environmental issues has become a focal point of global attention. This section explores the growing role of philanthropy in addressing climate change, promoting environmental sustainability, and supporting initiatives that seek to preserve and protect the planet. How can philanthropy be a driving force for positive environmental impact in the face of pressing ecological challenges?

Inclusive and Equitable Philanthropy

An increasing emphasis on inclusivity and equity is reshaping the philanthropic landscape. This section examines the importance of fostering diversity in philanthropic leadership, amplifying marginalized voices, and addressing systemic inequalities. How can philanthropy contribute to building a more inclusive and equitable world, and what strategies are being employed to ensure a broader representation of perspectives in decision-making?

Global Health Security and Pandemic Preparedness

Recent global events have underscored the importance of health security and pandemic preparedness. This section explores the role of philanthropy in supporting initiatives that enhance global health infrastructure, address public health crises, and ensure equitable access to healthcare. How can philanthropy contribute to building resilient health systems and responding effectively to future pandemics?

The Ethical Compass of Philanthropy

Ethical considerations play a crucial role in the future of philanthropy. This section reflects on the ethical challenges that may arise as philanthropy continues to evolve, including issues related to power dynamics, transparency, and accountability. How can philanthropists navigate these ethical complexities, and what frameworks and standards can guide ethical decision-making in the philanthropic sector?

Conclusion: Paving the Way Forward

As we conclude this exploration of the future of philanthropy, the chapter offers reflections on the potential paths forward. It considers how individuals, families, and organizations can draw inspiration from the lessons of the past and present to shape a future where philanthropy becomes an even more potent force for positive change. The conclusion serves as a call to action, inviting readers to contribute to the ongoing narrative of philanthropy in a world that continues to evolve and present new opportunities and challenges.

10

Reflections and Action: Incorporating Lessons from Francoise Bettencourt Meyers

Introduction

In this final chapter, we engage in a process of reflection and action, drawing on the lessons gleaned from the life and philanthropy of Francoise Bettencourt Meyers. As we navigate the insights provided throughout this exploration, we consider how these lessons can inform our own actions and contributions to the evolving landscape of wealth, inheritance, and philanthropy.

Reflecting on Personal Values

At the core of Bettencourt Meyers' philanthropic journey are her deeply ingrained values. This section encourages readers to reflect on their own values, beliefs, and principles that may guide their approach to wealth and philanthropy. What are the core values that drive personal decisions, and how can these values be translated into meaningful and impactful philanthropic endeavors?

Balancing Wealth and Responsibility

The delicate balance between wealth and responsibility is a recurring theme in the life of Francoise Bettencourt Meyers. This section prompts readers to reflect on their own relationships with wealth, considering the responsibilities and ethical considerations that come with financial privilege. How can individuals navigate the complexities of wealth stewardship while embracing a sense of social and moral duty?

Embracing Strategic Philanthropy

Bettencourt Meyers' strategic approach to philanthropy is a key element of her impact. This section explores the concept of strategic philanthropy and invites readers to consider how a thoughtful and intentional approach to giving can enhance the effectiveness of their contributions. What causes align with personal values, and how can philanthropy be leveraged to create sustainable and positive change?

Fostering Collaboration and Partnerships

Collaboration has been a cornerstone of Bettencourt Meyers' philanthropic success. This section encourages readers to explore the potential for collaboration and partnerships in their own philanthropic efforts. How can individuals, families, and organizations work together to amplify their impact and address complex societal challenges more effectively?

Building a Lasting Legacy

Consideration of legacy is integral to the philanthropic journey. This section prompts readers to contemplate the kind of legacy they wish to leave behind. What values, principles, and contributions will endure over time? How can individuals ensure that their philanthropy creates a lasting and positive impact on the world?

Addressing Contemporary Challenges

The challenges faced by Bettencourt Meyers offer valuable lessons for navigating the complexities of philanthropy. This section encourages readers to reflect on contemporary challenges, both global and local, and consider how their philanthropic efforts can contribute to addressing pressing issues such as inequality, environmental degradation, and public health crises.

Taking Action: A Call to Philanthropy

The chapter concludes with a call to action, motivating readers to translate reflections into meaningful philanthropic initiatives. It provides practical steps for individuals, families, and organizations to embark on their philanthropic journeys, emphasizing the idea that every action, no matter how small, can contribute to positive change. The call to philanthropy challenges readers to actively participate in shaping a future where giving becomes an integral part of creating a better world for all.

Incorporating these reflections and lessons into personal and collective philanthropic endeavors, readers have the opportunity to contribute to the ongoing narrative of wealth, inheritance, and philanthropy in ways that align with their values, make a lasting impact, and shape a more compassionate and equitable future.

11

The Everlasting Tapestry of Giving

Introduction

As we reach the final chapter of our exploration, we embark on a contemplative journey into the everlasting tapestry of giving. Drawing inspiration from the life and philanthropy of Francoise Bettencourt Meyers, this chapter invites readers to reflect on the interconnected threads of wealth, inheritance, and philanthropy, weaving a narrative that spans generations and leaves an indelible mark on the world.

Weaving the Threads of Inheritance

The chapter begins by weaving the threads of inheritance, tracing the complex tapestry of familial legacies and the responsibilities entwined with the passing of wealth from one generation to the next. It explores how individuals navigate the intricate patterns of inheritance, acknowledging the influence of cultural, ethical, and familial considerations on the fabric of their financial legacies.

The Philanthropic Thread: A Tapestry of Impact

Central to the narrative is the philanthropic thread, which brings vibrancy and purpose to the tapestry of giving. The chapter delves into the myriad ways in which philanthropy can be woven into the fabric of personal and familial legacies. It explores the transformative impact that intentional giving can have on individuals, communities, and the broader societal landscape.

Lessons from the Loom: Insights from Francoise Bettencourt Meyers

Building on the insights gleaned from the life of Francoise Bettencourt Meyers, this section distills key lessons from her philanthropic journey. It reflects on the strategic and intentional choices she made, the challenges she navigated, and the enduring legacy she has crafted. These lessons serve as a guide for readers as they contemplate their own roles within the evolving tapestry of giving.

The Interwoven Threads of Global Philanthropy

Expanding the narrative, the chapter explores the interwoven threads of global philanthropy. It reflects on the interconnectedness of philanthropic efforts around the world, acknowledging that the impact of giving extends far beyond individual borders. The tapestry of global philanthropy is shaped by shared challenges, collaborative endeavors, and the collective aspiration for positive change.

Nurturing the Seeds of Future Giving

The chapter contemplates the future of philanthropy, envisioning the seeds planted today that will blossom into meaningful contributions in the years to come. It encourages readers to consider how they can nurture a culture of giving within their families, organizations, and communities, ensuring that the tapestry of philanthropy continues to evolve and thrive.

Epilogue: A Tapestry Unfolding

In the epilogue, the chapter reflects on the ongoing narrative of philanthropy as a tapestry continually unfolding. It emphasizes that each act of giving, no matter how small, contributes to the richness and complexity of the overall narrative. The epilogue invites readers to recognize their role in this unfolding tapestry and to appreciate the collective impact of individual threads woven together.

Closing Thoughts: A Tapestry of Possibilities

As the book draws to a close, the final chapter offers closing thoughts on the tapestry of possibilities that philanthropy presents. It underscores the potential for individuals to shape a meaningful and enduring legacy through intentional giving. The chapter concludes with an invitation for readers to actively participate in the ongoing creation of a tapestry that reflects their values, aspirations, and commitment to a better world.

12

A Call to Action: Sustaining the Legacy of Giving

Introduction

In this concluding chapter, we issue a resounding call to action, recognizing the power of individual agency and collective efforts in sustaining the legacy of giving. Drawing inspiration from the philanthropic journey of Francoise Bettencourt Meyers, we explore concrete steps, initiatives, and a mindset that can foster a culture of sustained and impactful philanthropy.

Reflection on Personal Capacities

The chapter begins with a reflection on personal capacities, emphasizing that everyone, regardless of financial standing, possesses the ability to contribute to positive change. It explores the notion that philanthropy is not solely about monetary donations but encompasses the valuable resources of time, skills, and networks. Readers are encouraged to consider the unique capacities they can bring to the realm of giving.

Empowering Future Generations

Bettencourt Meyers' legacy is not only one of financial stewardship but also of passing down values and a sense of responsibility. This section delves into the importance of empowering future generations with the tools and mindset needed to continue a legacy of giving. It explores strategies for instilling philanthropic values in children and heirs, ensuring that the tapestry of giving endures.

Strategic Philanthropy: Leveraging Impact

Building on the strategic philanthropy exemplified by Bettencourt Meyers, this section emphasizes the importance of intentional giving. It explores how individuals and families can strategically align their philanthropic efforts with their values, leveraging impact in areas that resonate with their beliefs. The chapter provides insights into creating a philanthropic plan that maximizes positive outcomes.

Creating Collaborative Networks

Recognizing the interconnected nature of global challenges, this section advocates for the creation of collaborative networks. It explores the potential for individuals, organizations, and communities to join forces, pool resources, and collectively address complex issues. The chapter considers how collaboration can amplify impact, foster innovation, and lead to holistic solutions.

Embracing Innovation and Adaptability

In a rapidly changing world, the philanthropic landscape requires innovation and adaptability. This section explores how embracing new technologies, creative solutions, and adaptive strategies can enhance the effectiveness of philanthropic initiatives. It encourages readers to remain open to evolving approaches that respond dynamically to emerging challenges.

Promoting Diversity, Equity, and Inclusion

The chapter underscores the importance of promoting diversity, equity, and inclusion in philanthropy. It explores how cultivating a culture of inclusivity can lead to more comprehensive and equitable outcomes. The section advocates for philanthropy that actively addresses systemic inequalities and fosters positive change for marginalized communities.

Measuring Impact and Accountability

To ensure the sustainability of the legacy of giving, this section focuses on the critical aspects of measuring impact and accountability. It explores the role of effective evaluation, transparent reporting, and accountability mechanisms in philanthropy. The chapter encourages a continuous cycle of reflection, learning, and improvement to enhance the efficacy of giving.

Inspiration for Ongoing Giving

The chapter concludes by offering ongoing inspiration for sustained giving. It reflects on the enduring impact of consistent, intentional philanthropy and encourages readers to view giving as a lifelong commitment. The chapter reiterates the transformative potential of each act of generosity and calls on individuals to make a lasting imprint on the tapestry of giving.

Closing Thoughts: A Legacy in Motion

As we conclude this exploration, the chapter leaves readers with a sense of empowerment and responsibility. It emphasizes that the legacy of giving is not a static entity but a dynamic force that evolves with each intentional act of generosity. The chapter encourages readers to envision their philanthropic legacy as a legacy in motion, ever-changing and adapting to the needs of the world.

13

Forward Together: Shaping a Collective Philanthropic Future

Introduction

In this final chapter, we look forward together, recognizing that the future of philanthropy is a collective endeavor shaped by the actions of individuals, families, communities, and organizations. Building on the insights gained from the life and philanthropy of Francoise Bettencourt Meyers, this chapter explores the collaborative potential to create positive change on a global scale.

Philanthropy as a Shared Responsibility

The chapter begins by emphasizing that philanthropy is a shared responsibility that extends beyond individual actions. It explores the interconnectedness of giving and the collective impact that can be achieved when individuals and entities come together. Readers are invited to consider how a shared commitment to philanthropy can foster a sense of global responsibility.

Cultivating a Culture of Giving

Central to the discussion is the idea of cultivating a culture of giving within communities and organizations. This section explores the role of collective philanthropy in fostering a shared mindset of generosity, empathy, and social responsibility. It examines how a culture of giving can become ingrained in societal values, influencing future generations and creating a lasting legacy.

Global Challenges, Collaborative Solutions

Addressing the complexity of global challenges requires collaborative solutions. The chapter delves into the potential of cross-sector collaboration, where philanthropists, governments, businesses, and nonprofits work in tandem to tackle issues such as poverty, inequality, climate change, and health crises. It explores how diverse perspectives and resources can be harnessed for more comprehensive and sustainable solutions.

The Role of Innovative Partnerships

Innovation often thrives in partnerships, and this section explores the role of innovative collaborations in the future of philanthropy. It highlights examples of successful partnerships that have leveraged unique strengths and resources to address specific challenges. The chapter encourages the exploration of new and creative alliances to amplify the impact of philanthropic efforts.

Youth and the Next Generation of Philanthropists

As stewards of the future, the next generation plays a pivotal role in shaping the philanthropic landscape. This section explores the potential of youth-led initiatives and the importance of empowering young individuals to become philanthropists in their own right. It reflects on how supporting and mentoring the next generation can contribute to a sustainable and evolving culture of giving.

Adapting to Emerging Trends

The future of philanthropy is dynamic, influenced by emerging trends and evolving societal needs. This section examines how individuals and organizations can stay attuned to these trends, adapting their philanthropic strategies to remain relevant and effective. It explores the potential of staying ahead of the curve in addressing emerging challenges and opportunities.

Technology and Philanthropy: A Transformative Duo

Technology continues to be a driving force in shaping the future of philanthropy. This section explores the transformative potential of technology in facilitating charitable giving, enhancing transparency, and connecting philanthropists with impactful initiatives. It reflects on how embracing technological advancements can lead to more efficient, accessible, and innovative philanthropy.

Creating a Legacy of Unity and Impact

The chapter concludes by envisioning a future where the legacy of giving is marked by unity and impact. It emphasizes the collective responsibility to shape a philanthropic landscape that transcends individual contributions. The closing thoughts encourage readers to reflect on how their actions today can contribute to a legacy of shared responsibility, collaboration, and positive global impact.

In the spirit of Francoise Bettencourt Meyers' legacy, the chapter invites readers to join hands in forging a philanthropic future that reflects the collective commitment to creating positive change, leaving a lasting imprint on the tapestry of giving for generations to come.

14

Summary

"Inheritance and Philanthropy: A Closer Look at Francoise Bettencourt Meyers' Impact on Wealth and Giving" is a comprehensive exploration spanning twelve chapters. The book begins by introducing Francoise Bettencourt Meyers, an influential philanthropist, and delves into the intricate connection between wealth, inheritance, and her commitment to giving.

Chapters 1-3: The early chapters provide a detailed background on Francoise Bettencourt Meyers, her family's wealth, and the intertwining dynamics of inheritance and philanthropy. The narrative unfolds through the lens of her personal journey, shedding light on the influences that shaped her commitment to making a positive impact on the world.

Chapters 4-6: The middle chapters delve into the multifaceted aspects of Bettencourt Meyers' philanthropy. From education and environmental stewardship to health and social justice, the book explores the diverse causes she champions. It examines her strategic approach, the impact of her initiatives, and how she adapts to the evolving challenges of the global landscape.

Chapters 7-9: The narrative takes a reflective turn, examining the legacy and lessons derived from Bettencourt Meyers' philanthropic journey. It explores

SUMMARY

the ethical considerations, innovation in philanthropy, and the importance of measuring impact and accountability. Legacy building and succession planning also feature prominently in these chapters.

Chapter 10: The tenth chapter focuses on the concept of the "everlasting tapestry of giving," metaphorically weaving together inheritance, wealth, and philanthropy. It reflects on the interconnected threads of personal values, the transformative power of philanthropy, and the enduring lessons from Bettencourt Meyers' life.

Chapter 11: The penultimate chapter issues a "call to action," encouraging readers to actively contribute to sustaining the legacy of giving. It explores strategies for intentional philanthropy, fostering collaboration, embracing innovation, and promoting diversity and inclusion.

Chapter 12: The final chapter looks forward, envisioning a collective philanthropic future shaped by shared responsibility, a culture of giving, and collaboration. It explores the role of youth, the impact of technology, and the potential for creating a legacy of unity and positive global impact.

Overall Themes:
  - The book underscores the intricate relationship between inheritance, wealth, and philanthropy, using Francoise Bettencourt Meyers' life as a lens to explore these themes.
  - It emphasizes the strategic and intentional nature of philanthropy, encouraging readers to align their giving with their values for a lasting impact.
  - The importance of collaboration, adaptation to emerging trends, and the role of technology in shaping the future of philanthropy are recurring themes.
  - Legacy, both personal and collective, is a central focus, urging individuals to consider the enduring impact of their actions on the ever-evolving tapestry of giving.

www.ingramcontent.com/pod-product-compliance
Lightning Source LLC
LaVergne TN
LVHW020455080526
838202LV00057B/5964